Let's Discover Canada
YUKON

by
Suzanne LeVert

George Sheppard
McMaster University
General Editor

CHELSEA HOUSE PUBLISHERS
New York   Philadelphia

Cover: Emerald Lake, near Carcross
Opposite: Preparing for a snowmobile journey across the Yukon's rugged terrain

Chelsea House Publishers
EDITOR-IN-CHIEF: Remmel Nunn
MANAGING EDITOR: Karyn Gullen Browne
COPY CHIEF: Mark Rifkin
PICTURE EDITOR: Adrian G. Allen
ART DIRECTOR: Maria Epes
ASSISTANT ART DIRECTOR: Noreen Romano
MANUFACTURING DIRECTOR: Gerald Levine
SYSTEMS MANAGER: Lindsey Ottman
PRODUCTION MANAGER: Joseph Romano
PRODUCTION COORDINATOR: Marie Claire Cebrián

Let's Discover Canada
SENIOR EDITOR: Rebecca Stefoff

Staff for YUKON
COPY EDITOR: Benson D. Simmonds
EDITORIAL ASSISTANT: Ian Wilker
PICTURE RESEARCHER: Alan Gottlieb
DESIGNER: Diana Blume

First Printing

1   3   5   7   9   8   6   4   2

Library of Congress Cataloging-in-Publication Data
LeVert, Suzanne.
    Let's discover Canada. Yukon/by Suzanne LeVert.
      p. cm.
    Includes bibliographical references and index.
    Summary: Discusses the geography, history, and culture of Canada's Yukon Territory.
    ISBN 0-7910-1032-5
    1. Yukon Territory—Juvenile literature.   [1. Yukon Territory.] I. Title.
    F1091.4.L48   1992   91-20773
    971.9′1—dc20   CIP
                                           AC

Contents

My Canada

by Pierre Berton

"Nobody knows my country," a great Canadian journalist, Bruce Hutchison, wrote almost half a century ago. It is still true. Most Americans, I think, see Canada as a pleasant vacationland and not much more. And yet we are the United States's greatest single commercial customer, and the United States is our largest customer.

Lacking a major movie industry, we have made no wide-screen epics to chronicle our triumphs and our tragedies. But then there has been little blood in our colonial past—no revolutions, no civil war, not even a wild west. Yet our history is crammed with remarkable men and women. I am thinking of Joshua Slocum, the first man to sail alone around the world, and Robert Henderson, the prospector who helped start the Klondike gold rush. I am thinking of some of our famous artists and writers—comedian Dan Aykroyd, novelists Margaret Atwood and Robertson Davies, such popular performers as Michael J. Fox, Anne Murray, Gordon Lightfoot, and k.d. lang, and hockey greats from Maurice Richard to Gordie Howe to Wayne Gretzky.

The real shape of Canada explains why our greatest epic has been the building of the Pacific Railway to unite the nation from

The Yukon Territory, encompassing some of the wildest and least populated country in North America, is a paradise for outdoorspeople.

sea to sea in 1885. On the map, the country looks square. But because the overwhelming majority of Canadians live within 100 miles (160 kilometers) of the U.S. border, in practical terms the nation is long and skinny. We are in fact an archipelago of population islands separated by implacable barriers—the angry ocean, three mountain walls, and the Canadian Shield, that vast desert of billion-year-old rock that sprawls over half the country, rich in mineral treasures, impossible for agriculture.

Canada's geography makes the country difficult to govern and explains our obsession with transportation and communication. The government has to be as involved in railways, airlines, and broadcasting networks as it is with social services such as universal medical care. Rugged individualism is not a Canadian quality. Given the environment, people long ago learned to work together for security.

It is ironic that the very bulwarks that separate us—the chiseled peaks of the Selkirk Mountains, the gnarled scarps north of Lake Superior, the ice-choked waters of the Northumberland Strait —should also be among our greatest attractions for tourists and artists. But if that is the paradox of Canada, it is also the glory.

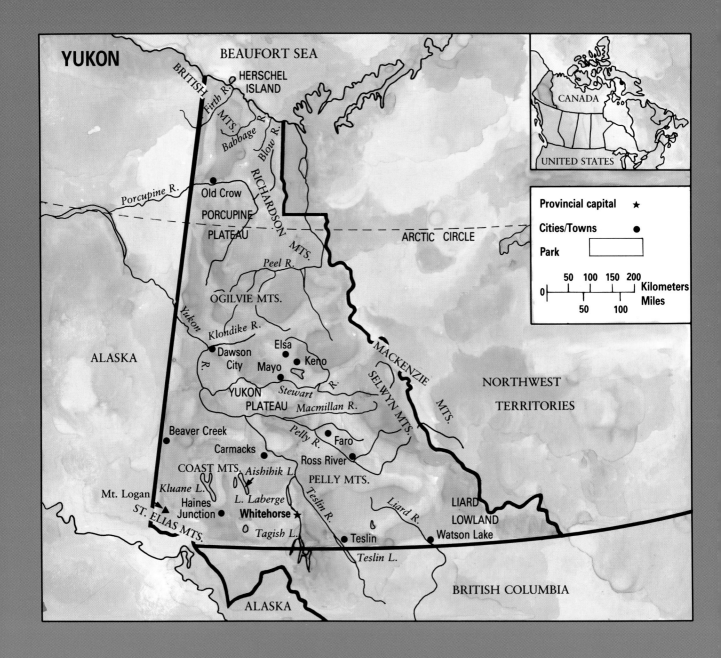

YUKON

BEAUFORT SEA

BRITISH
Firth R.
HERSCHEL
ISLAND

RICHARDSON
MTS.
Babbage R.
Blow R.

Porcupine R.
Old Crow
PORCUPINE
PLATEAU

ARCTIC CIRCLE

Peel R.

MTS.

OGILVIE MTS.

Yukon R.
Klondike R.
Dawson
City
Elsa
Keno
Mayo

ALASKA

YUKON
PLATEAU
Stewart R.
Macmillan R.

SELWYN MTS.

MACKENZIE
MTS.

NORTHWEST

TERRITORIES

Beaver Creek
Pelly R.
Faro
Carmacks
Ross River
PELLY MTS.

COAST MTS.
Aishihik L.
Kluane L.
Mt. Logan
Haines
Junction
L. Laberge
Whitehorse ★
Teslin R.
Liard R.
LIARD
LOWLAND

ST. ELIAS MTS.
Tagish L.
Teslin
Watson Lake
Teslin L.

ALASKA
BRITISH COLUMBIA

CANADA
UNITED STATES

Provincial capital ★
Cities/Towns ●
Park ▭

0   50   100   150   200   Kilometers
                              Miles
0   50   100

Yukon at a Glance

Population: 30,000 in 1989

Area: 186,660 square miles (483,450 square kilometers)

Capital: Whitehorse (population 20,706)

Other cities: Dawson City (population 1,791), Watson Lake (population 1,744), Faro (population 1,606), Haines Junction (population 642), Mayo (population 500)

Entered Dominion of Canada: June 13, 1898

Principal products: Lead, zinc, gold, silver, lumber

Principal industries: Mining, tourism, foresty

Provincial flower: Fireweed

Provincial bird: Raven

Provincial coat of arms: A shield surmounted by a malamute dog. The red-and-white cross of St. James represents English explorers; a circle in the cross represents the fur trade; red triangles with gold circles represent mineral-rich mountains; wavy stripes represent rivers; and the dog represents the northland.

Government: A commissioner is appointed by the federal government; the territory's executive branch is headed by an official called the government leader, who leads the majority party in the territory's 16-member legislative assembly and oversees a cabinet of 5 members, also chosen from the assembly; one senator and one member of the House of Commons represent the Yukon in the federal government.

The Land

The Yukon Territory, located in Canada's far northwest, is a tract of rugged, largely uninhabited land the size of France. With its high peaks, gleaming glaciers, and winding rivers, the Yukon contains some of North America's most magnificent arctic landscapes. It is one of the coldest regions in the world, a land of long, dark winters and harsh blizzards. Yet during the brief spring the Yukon is carpeted with colorful wildflowers, and in autumn its mountainsides and valleys are covered with the shimmering gold of aspen leaves.

Roughly triangular in shape, the Yukon Territory has an area of 186,660 square miles (483,450 square kilometers). It is bordered by the province of British Columbia on the south, the state of Alaska on the southwest and west, and the Northwest Territories on the east. On the north it faces the Beaufort Sea, part of the Arctic Ocean. The Yukon Territory also includes Herschel Island, an uninhabited 39-square-mile (100-square-kilometer) island in the Beaufort Sea. The Arctic Circle cuts across the northern Yukon; the northern tip of the territory is in the Arctic zone.

Opposite: Hikers overlook a glacier in Kluane National Park in the St. Elias Mountains. Kluane is the largest mountain park in Canada; its magnificent landscape of peaks, gorges, lakes, and ice fields has been named a World Heritage Site by the United Nations.
Above: Dall sheep live among the mountain crags, foraging for mosses, flowers, and hardy grasses. Despite their substantial size, they can leap nimbly up and down even the steepest slopes.

The Yukon has three kinds of terrain: mountain ranges, plateaus, and coastal tundra. The mountains are the northernmost extension of the mighty cordillera, or mountain system, that runs from north to south throughout western North America. In the southwestern corner of the Yukon are the high, icy, jagged St. Elias Mountains, which straddle the border with Alaska. The southern Yukon has the Coast and Pelly ranges; the western Yukon has the low, rounded Ogilvie Mountains; and the British Mountains separate the central Yukon from the northern coast. On the east, the steep Richardson, Selwyn, and Mackenzie ranges run along the Yukon's border with the Northwest Territories. Canada's highest mountain, Mt. Logan, is located in the St. Elias Range; it has an elevation of 19,850 feet (6,050 meters). Six other St. Elias peaks reach heights of 15,000 feet (4,572 meters) or more, and a total of 20 peaks in the Yukon are above 10,000 feet (3,000 meters). The St. Elias Range also contains the largest nonpolar ice field in North America. In the heart of the mountain range, the ice field is thought to be 2,300 feet (700 meters) thick. Glaciers up to 19 miles (30 kilometers) long extend down the valleys from the central ice field.

Between the mountain ranges, the Yukon consists of rolling, elevated plateaus, intersected by powerful rivers that have carved deep valleys. Between the Coast Range on the west and the Ogilvie and Selwyn ranges on the east lies a broad basin called the Yukon Plateau; the western part of this plateau, near the Alaska border and south of the Ogilvie Mountains, is called the Klondike after the Klondike River, which flows through it. In the southeast is the Liard Lowland, a low-lying gap between the mountains of British Columbia and the Yukon. North of the Ogilvie Mountains lies the Porcupine Plateau.

The northern edge of the Yukon consists of a narrow plain between the uplands of the interior and the 124-mile-long (200-kilometer-long) coastline on the icy Beaufort Sea. This coastal plain is tundra—that is, it is too far north for trees to grow but is covered by mosses, flowers, and low shrubs.

Much of the Yukon, especially in the north, is underlaid by permafrost, ground that remains frozen year-round. In permafrost

The Yukon River sweeps past Five Finger Rapids. Canada's second longest river flows from British Columbia across the Yukon Territory before winding through Alaska to empty into the Bering Sea. Its banks are dotted with crumbling log cabins that date from the early 20th century, relics of a time when the river was the highroad for trade in the region.

regions, the thin upper layer of soil that undergoes seasonal freezing and thawing is called the active layer; below it is the permafrost. When the active layer thaws during the summer, the underlying permafrost does not absorb the water that lies on the surface in hundreds of swamps and bogs. These wet, spongy areas are breeding grounds for trillions of black flies and mosquitoes, the scourges of the northern summer.

Waterways

The Yukon Territory is named after its most important river, the Yukon, which drains almost two-thirds of the territory. It is the second longest river in Canada (after the Mackenzie) and the fifth longest in North America. From its headwaters in British Columbia it runs for 1,979 miles (3,185 kilometers) northwest through the Yukon and Alaska to the Bering Sea. The largest lakes in the Yukon—Teslin, Kluane, Laberge, Aishihik, and Tagish—are near the Yukon's headwaters.

The territory has many other important rivers. The Liard River rises in the Pelly Mountains and flows into British Columbia before joining the Mackenzie River in the Northwest

A black bear ambles along a riverbank. Black bears are numerous in the forested southern Yukon; grizzly bears, their endangered cousins, prefer more open mountain terrain.

Territories. Other rivers include the Peel, which drains eastward into the Mackenzie; the Alsek, which flows through the St. Elias Range into the Gulf of Alaska; and the Firth, Babbage, and Blow rivers, which drain the coastal plain and empty into the Beaufort Sea. The Pelly, Teslin, Macmillan, Stewart, Klondike, and White rivers are tributaries of the Yukon.

Plant and Animal Life

Cold temperatures and permafrost mean that the Yukon has little productive farmland. Approximately 57 percent of the territory is forested, but only 15 percent of the forested land can be considered useful for commercial tree harvesting. The Yukon's forests are of a type called subarctic boreal forest, which consists of stands of pine, aspen, poplar, and birch trees. Trees in boreal forests grow much more slowly than those at lower latitudes, so that many decades may be needed to replace cut trees. The Yukon's densest forests and tallest trees are found south of Dawson City and in the Liard Lowland.

The Yukon has fur-bearing animals—beavers, foxes, wolverines, martens, and muskrats—as well as black bears, moose, elk, and wolves. Grizzly bears, an endangered species, are found throughout the Yukon; Kluane National Park has the world's largest concentration of these immense bears. The territory also has many Dall sheep, whose large, curling horns are highly prized trophies for big-game hunters. A caribou herd called the Porcupine herd, which includes about 165,000 animals and is one of the world's biggest herds of barren-ground caribou, migrates annually across the territory. Once hunted almost to extinction, the caribou are now protected by hunting limits. The traditional way of life of the Yukon's Native peoples still depends heavily upon the meat and skins of the caribou.

The northern part of the Yukon is home to several Arctic mammals: musk-oxen and polar bears on land and seals, walrus, and beluga and bowhead whales in the sea. At the end of the 19th century, whaling was one of the Yukon's most important economic activities, attracting whalers from around the world. Herschel Island, the only sheltered harbor along the territory's Arctic coast, was a base for whaling camps.

The Yukon's coastal waters and its thousands of lakes and streams are filled with fish—arctic grayling, pacific salmon, lake trout, whitefish, northern pike, and arctic char, a fish similar to salmon. The birds of the Yukon include ravens, bald and golden eagles, boreal owls, hawks, peregrine falcons, gyrfalcons, grouse, and ptarmigan. Many species of migratory birds, including trumpeter and tundra swans, snow geese, sandhill cranes, and several species of ducks, spend summers raising their young in the Yukon and then fly south to warmer climes for the winter.

Climate

During its long, dark winters, the Yukon is one of the coldest places on earth, partly because it is so far north and partly because the St. Elias and Coast mountains prevent warmer Pacific air from reaching the interior of the territory. One of the lowest temperatures ever recorded in North America, −81 degrees Fahrenheit (−63 degrees Celsius), occurred in the western Yukon in February 1947. Average January temperatures are 5°F (−15°C) in Whitehorse and −16°F (−27°C) in Dawson City. The Yukon's summers, though brief, are mild, with average temperatures of about 50°F (10°C) in the north and 60°F (16°C) in the south. The territory's record high temperature of 95°F (35°C) occurred in Dawson City and Mayo in June 1950.

The Yukon receives about 40 inches (100 centimeters) of snow each year in the north and more than twice that much in

Mt. Logan, Canada's highest peak, rises to a height of 19,850 feet (6,050 meters) above the tumbled ice and rock of the St. Elias range in the southeastern Yukon.

the south. Annual rainfall ranges from 9 to 13 inches (23 to 33 centimeters).

One of the most fascinating aspects of life above the Arctic Circle is the phenomenon called the midnight sun. During the Yukon summer, days are extremely long. At midsummer the sun does not set at all: The southern part of the territory has a week of round-the-clock daylight, and in the north, the sun remains above the horizon for two months. The long summer days produce a carpet of colorful wildflowers and allow vegetables grown in both greenhouses and gardens to reach unusually large sizes. The opposite of the midnight sun occurs during the northern winter, when the days are short and the nights are long. Some parts of the southern Yukon receive only about 6.5 hours of daylight each day in January, and north of the Arctic Circle the sun does not appear at all for several months.

The darkness of winter brings one spectacular advantage: Winter is the best time for viewing the aurora borealis, or northern lights, in the night skies above the Yukon and the Northwest Territories. Streams and bands of glowing green, red, and purple light swirl in the sky. They originate in the upper atmosphere and are caused by electromagnetic activity among air molecules. The kaleidoscope of the northern lights in the night sky is one of nature's most extravagant wonders.

The History

Archaeologists believe that Native American peoples came from northeastern Asia and may have reached the Yukon as many as 20,000 years ago. During the ice ages thousands of years ago, when the polar ice caps were more extensive than they are today and the level of the world's oceans was lower, Siberia and Alaska were connected by a land bridge where the Bering Strait now lies. Nomadic hunters, following the bison and woolly mammoth, eventually made their way from Asia through present-day Alaska into the Yukon and the rest of the Americas.

Archaeologists, who study the physical traces of human activity in the past, and anthropologists, who study human cultures, have found that the Yukon Natives' culture belongs to a large family of related languages and traditions called Athapaskan; some of the Natives of Alaska and the Northwest Territories are also members of this family. The Athapaskan culture as it exists today was well established in the Yukon by at least A.D. 800.

Opposite: The Yukon first came to the attention of the outside world when gold was discovered there in 1896. Thousands of hopeful prospectors, laden with food and supplies, struggled up the steep, icy Chilkoot Pass to cross from Skagway, Alaska, into the Yukon.
Above: The North West Mounted Police, later called the Royal Canadian Mounted Police, was charged with keeping the peace during the gold rush. These Mounties were photographed outside their Dawson City post in 1900.

The Native inhabitants of the Yukon belonged to several different cultural groups, but each had adapted ways of surviving in the cold, harsh climate. The manufacture of warm clothing from animal hides was an important skill.

Five major Athapaskan-speaking peoples lived in the Yukon. They were the Gwich'in (sometimes called Kutchin or Loucheux), Han, Tutchone, Kaska, and Tagish. Each of these groups spoke its own version of the ancestral Athapaskan language, and each lived in a different part of what is now the Yukon Territory. The Gwich'in were the northernmost group, living along the Peel and Porcupine rivers. They were nomadic, following the migratory caribou herds. The Han lived along the Yukon River and its tributaries north of present-day Dawson City, fishing salmon from the river in the summer and hunting game in the winter. The Tutchone lived in the central Yukon region, from Kluane Lake in the southwest north to the Ogilvie and Selwyn mountains. They were seasonal hunters, fishing for salmon and whitefish during the summer and hunting caribou, moose, and Dall sheep later in the year. The Kaska, a hunting people, lived in the mountainous areas at the headwaters of the Pelly and Liard rivers in the southeastern Yukon. The Tagish were hunters and fishers who lived around the southern lakes. Today many of the members of each group live in cities, towns, or villages in their traditional homelands.

In addition to the Athapaskan-speaking peoples, some non-Athapaskan Natives inhabited the Yukon. A few Inuit, belonging to the culture and language group—formerly called Eskimos—that spread along the Arctic coast from Alaska to Hudson Bay, lived on the coast of the Beaufort Sea and on Herschel Island. They hunted caribou on the tundra and seals and walrus on the sea ice. And in the 19th century the Tlingit, a Native group from the Alaskan coast, began to migrate into the southern Yukon. They arranged trading partnerships and marriages with the Yukon Natives and settled south of the present-day capital city of Whitehorse.

The Yukon's Native peoples did not organize themselves into tribes or political units. They lived in bands of 20 to 25 people, usually members of an extended family. Each small band struggled to survive in the subarctic wilderness. The pattern of their lives was set by the availability and movements of food sources: In the winter, they hunted in the forests, and in the summer, they fished in the lakes and rivers. They also gathered wild berries, which were dried to be eaten during the winter or pounded and combined with grease and meat to make the easily preserved food called pemmican. Although they did not have a formal tribal structure, the Natives did have contact with other members of their language groups. It is likely that each of the scattered family bands encountered members of the other bands at some time during the course of each year while moving between campsites or foraging for food. People could leave one band to join another; this is how marriages were arranged.

Native society was egalitarian and promoted individuality and self-reliance. Because of their nomadic way of life, the Natives did not accumulate personal possessions: Most tools and even houses were made with the materials at hand rather than carried from place to place. The Athapaskan-speaking Natives admired an individual for his or her skill at adapting to the demanding conditions of subarctic life. They also had deeply felt religious convictions. They believed that animals, rivers, the weather, and most other natural phenomena were inhabited or controlled by powerful spirits. Religious leaders called shamans attempted to control the spirit powers. It was thought that a shaman could intercede with the spirits to change the weather, locate game, and cure the sick.

One important cultural tradition was shared by all the Athapaskan-speaking groups of the Yukon. They divided all of society into two clans, the Crow and the Wolf. Clan membership was hereditary, passing from mother to children. It helped define an individual's place in society and his or her duties and responsibilities to others. Tradition held that Crow men must marry Wolf women and that Wolf men must marry Crow women; this promoted ties between the clans. Clan identity remains strong today among the Yukon Natives.

The Northwest Passage and the Fur Trade

The Yukon was one of the last parts of the New World to be explored by Europeans. By the 18th century, Russian fur traders were spreading into Alaska and reaching eastward toward the Yukon. The fur trade also approached the Yukon from the

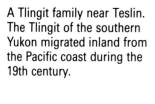

A Tlingit family near Teslin. The Tlingit of the southern Yukon migrated inland from the Pacific coast during the 19th century.

southeast. In 1789 a Scottish explorer named Alexander Mackenzie, working for a fur-trading company, traveled north from central Canada through the present-day Northwest Territories along the river that now bears his name. He was told by the local Natives that there was a second great river in the west, beyond the mountains—the Yukon River. Although Mackenzie did not see the Yukon, he reported the rumors of its existence.

The Yukon Territory did not become known to Europeans until the early 19th century, when Sir John Franklin, a captain in the British Royal Navy, was asked by the British government to map North America's unknown Arctic seaboard. The British hoped that Franklin's venture would serve three purposes: to limit Russia's activities in the Arctic, to promote geography and other natural sciences, and, perhaps most important, to find the Northwest Passage, the sea route from the Atlantic Ocean to the Pacific Ocean that was believed to cross North America. Explorers had been searching for the Northwest Passage almost since the first European mariners reached North America.

Franklin made three Arctic trips. On his second journey, in 1825, he sailed north on the Mackenzie River with four ships. When he reached the Beaufort Sea, he sent two ships eastward to map the shoreline of the Northwest Territories. He took the other ships westward along the coast, surveying about 400 miles (640 kilometers) of the ice-fringed, fogbound shore, including the coast of what is now the Yukon. Years later he undertook a third expedition in search of the Northwest Passage; he and all his men died when their ships were frozen solid in the Arctic ice.

By the mid-19th century, however, the exploration of the interior of northwestern Canada and the exploitation of its resources had become almost as important to the Europeans as the discovery of the Northwest Passage. The principal force in opening up the interior was the Hudson's Bay Company (HBC), a large and powerful trading firm that had been founded in 1670 to export furs and other goods from Canada. The British government, which had claimed most of Canada, turned over an enormous tract of territory to the HBC. That territory was called

Sir John Franklin explored the Yukon coast before his fateful attempt to sail the Northwest Passage. His ships were lost in the 1840s, but the explorers who searched for him succeeded at last in conquering the elusive passage.

Prince Rupert's Land, and it originally included present-day northern Quebec and Ontario, all of Manitoba, most of Saskatchewan, southern Alberta, and the adjoining territory to the north and west.

From its first stockades and trading posts on the shores of Hudson Bay, the HBC worked its way into the heart of the continent, developing the fur trade as it went. HBC agents encouraged the Natives to trap and hunt fur-bearing animals and trade the pelts for blankets, guns, liquor, food, and other goods. The company's tireless traders were often followed by missionaries, hunters, soldiers, and eventually settlers.

The HBC sent its first emissaries into the Yukon in the 1840s. After establishing the company's northernmost post on the eastern bank of the Peel River in what is now the Northwest Territories, John Bell crossed the Yukon Territory. He was the first European to reach the junction of the Yukon and Porcupine rivers in present-day Alaska. Fort Yukon was established there. Robert Campbell spent the years 1840–48 exploring the Liard and Pelly rivers and the headwaters of the Yukon River. He founded Fort Selkirk at the junction of the Pelly and Yukon rivers.

Some of the Yukon Natives, with trading monopolies of their own to protect, viewed the arrival of the HBC with alarm. Both the Gwich'in and the Tlingit were accustomed to obtaining pelts from other Native groups to trade with the Russians, and they did not want rivals. The Tlingit attacked Fort Selkirk in 1852; other HBC outposts encountered similar hostility. The HBC gradually abandoned the southern Yukon in the 1850s. It was forced to give up Fort Yukon as well when the United States bought Alaska from Russia in 1867 and it was determined that Fort Yukon was located in American territory.

During the later part of the 19th century, a few traders trickled into the Yukon and set up small camps along the Yukon, Porcupine, and Pelly rivers. Farther north, along the coast, seamen arrived to hunt beluga and bowhead whales in the Beaufort Sea. Hundreds of whalers wintered on Herschel Island each year. They traded for furs, walrus ivory, and other goods with the Inuit of the Beaufort coast; they also introduced alcoholism and deadly new diseases, such as smallpox and measles, to the Inuit population.

A different kind of influence was exercised by the missionaries who were active in the Yukon after the 1860s. Reverend Robert McDonald of the Anglican church came to the Yukon in 1862 and remained for more than 40 years; he translated the Bible into the Gwich'in language. Bishop William Bompass, another Anglican, built many schools in the Yukon before his death in 1906.

The Nation of Canada

Although the development of the Canadian north proceeded slowly, the British colonies in eastern Canada grew in population and power throughout the first part of the 19th century. By the 1860s, Canada wanted to control and develop the prairie regions of the central plains as well, and it became clear that the Hudson's Bay Company could no longer control the people and resources of Prince Rupert's Land. The British, fearing that the United States might try to take over this poorly administered territory, bought Prince Rupert's Land back from the HBC to make it part of Canada.

A fur trapper with his catch

Independence from Britain came in 1867, when the British North America Act established the Dominion of Canada. The Dominion originally consisted of four provinces: Ontario, Quebec, New Brunswick, and Nova Scotia. A provision of the act, however, guaranteed that Prince Rupert's Land and the territory adjoining it on the northwest would also become part of Canada. In 1869, the Hudson's Bay Company gave up its claim to Prince Rupert's Land, and in 1870 the Canadian government divided the newly acquired land into the province of Manitoba and a much larger region called the North West Territories.

In 1882, four administrative districts were carved out of the territories; all were located in the prairie region of central Canada. Later, when people moved into the north, other districts were added. In 1895, a district called the Yukon was created in the northwestern corner of the territories. This administrative district had approximately the same boundaries as the Yukon Territory has today.

At the time the district was created, the Yukon had a small population—a few thousand Natives and fewer Europeans. Yet enough fur traders and mineral prospectors had arrived in the Yukon to prompt Canada's federal government in Ottawa to send a detachment of the North West Mounted Police (NWMP), commonly called the Mounties, to keep the peace. Federal administrative departments were set up in Dawson City, the district capital. In the years that followed, the government would be grateful for this administrative head start, for the Yukon was on the verge of a period of explosive growth—and the biggest gold rush in history.

The Klondike Gold Rush

Gold had been discovered in British Columbia in the mid-19th century, and a few gold-hungry prospectors moved north into the Yukon in the 1860s and 1870s. By the 1880s, gold nuggets and dust were being taken from the Stewart River and the lower Yukon, and a handful of stores opened in the region to supply the miners. But the big strike came in the 1890s.

In 1893, a man named George Washington Carmack built a log cabin on the banks of the Yukon River, about 108 miles (175 kilometers) north of where the city of Whitehorse stands today. Carmack traded with the local Natives for furs and did some prospecting, discovering coal near his cabin in 1896. That discovery was soon forgotten, for not long after finding the coal, he was given the tip of a lifetime. A fellow prospector named Robert Henderson told Carmack that gold could be found to the north, in the hills near the Klondike River.

Following Henderson's directions, Carmack and two Native American companions, Skookum Jim and Tagish Charlie, reached the Klondike. In a stream called Rabbit Creek, which flowed into the Klondike just east of the present-day site of Dawson City, they struck gold—a wealth of nuggets and gold dust, just lying in the streambed, waiting to be lifted and sifted out of the water. Rabbit Creek was renamed Bonanza Creek.

Word of Carmack's strike spread quickly through the Yukon. Prospectors already in the area staked claims to every creek along the Klondike River. Many of them found gold nuggets by the

At the close of one gold rush season, the Yukon River steamboat *Bonanza King* prepares to leave Dawson City for the trip south through the White Horse Rapids.

George Washington Carmack, whose find in Bonanza Creek launched the gold rush and brought fame to the Klondike

handful. The Klondike region would prove to be one of the richest sources of gold in North America.

In 1897, a steamer loaded with Yukon gold put into port at Seattle. After an enthusiastic article was published in the Seattle *Post-Intelligencer* describing the "ton of gold" that a prospector could find in the Klondike, the stampede was on. The gold rush that followed brought a total of perhaps 100,000 people from all over North America and Europe. During a few feverish years they swarmed into the subarctic wilderness in search of their fortunes.

The Klondike prospectors had to overcome many obstacles before they could even begin their search for gold. Half the battle was getting to the Klondike, conquering treacherous terrain and combating freezing temperatures. The most frequently used route began in Skagway, Alaska. The first hurdle was the Chilkoot Pass over the mountains on the border between Alaska and British Columbia. Climbing the steep, icy cliff to the 3,520-foot-high (1,073-meter-high) pass required strong muscles and nerves of steel. As if climbing the pass once were not difficult enough, most would-be prospectors had to climb it many times, because the NWMP established a post at the pass in 1897 and required that each prospector carry enough supplies for a full year in the wilderness. Some prospectors spent weeks climbing up and down the steep hill, assembling the required 1,760 pounds (800 kilograms) of supplies. Despite the difficulty, more than 30,000 crossed the pass in 1897 and 1898. By 1900, however, a narrow-gauge railway had been laid over the mountains from Skagway to Whitehorse in the Yukon.

Once over the pass, prospectors traveled across miles of forbidding countryside to Bennett Lake in British Columbia. There they cut down trees and built rafts and boats for the journey north on the fast-flowing waters of the Yukon River. Floating was easier than climbing and walking, but the river journey had its own dangers. Miles Canyon and the White Horse Rapids were just two of the tricky channels that had to be navigated. More than 7,100 canoes, steamers, and rafts had left Bennett Lake for the north by May 1898; at least 100 of them were wrecked at the canyon or the rapids.

Voyagers who survived the White Horse Rapids—where the city of Whitehorse is currently located—had to travel another 330 miles (530 kilometers) to Dawson City. Before the gold rush, Dawson City was a tiny frontier outpost. During May 1898, when the first big batch of prospectors arrived, it mushroomed into North America's largest city west of Winnipeg and north of San Francisco, with a population of 40,000 and a hastily erected profusion of hotels, boardinghouses, and tents to accommodate the newcomers. The streets of Dawson were lined with the wooden storefronts of saloons, dance halls, and casinos.

Along with the population boom came a certain amount of trouble. Brawls, thefts, and disputes over land claims and women were common in the rough-and-tumble Klondike. In 1898, the Canadian government sent the Yukon Field Force to Fort Selkirk, the former Hudson's Bay Company trading post. Composed of 203 officers and men from the Canadian militia, the Yukon Field

The gold rush turned Dawson City into a boomtown in the heart of the wilderness. Saloons, dance halls, and casinos sprang up overnight.

Force became a symbol of Canadian sovereignty and the rule of law on Canada's wild frontier. That same year, the Yukon administrative district of the North West Territories was made a separate territory, with Dawson City as its capital.

Around this time, the U.S. and Canadian governments were arguing over the precise location of the Alaska-Yukon border. Canada wanted the Yukon to have a seaport on the Pacific coast, but in 1903 an international commission ruled that the Alaskan panhandle—the strip of Alaska that runs south along the Pacific to British Columbia—belonged to the United States, and the Yukon was cut off from the Pacific.

The gold rush lasted for seven years, although the most profitable years were the first two. Nearly all of the major finds were made by the prospectors who were first on the scene; most latecomers found little or no gold. But the lure of gold kept drawing men—and some women—to the Yukon even after most of the surface gold had been removed. It is estimated that more than $100 million in gold was taken from the creeks of the Klondike between 1897 and 1904. During that time, the territory's permanent population grew to a high of perhaps 40,000. Many of those who did not strike it rich in the goldfields managed to prosper by opening businesses that provided goods and services to the prospectors.

The 20th Century

When the gold rush drew to an end, the population began to fall. In 1901, there were 27,000 people in the territory, but only 8,500 were left by 1911. The flood of prospectors ebbed, and people left the Yukon to seek their fortunes elsewhere. Some gold and silver mining continued in the territory, but little of the profit made during the gold rush had been invested in the Yukon. With no new industries to replace the gold rush, the Yukon slipped into a steady decline. In 1931, just 4,300 people remained in the territory; Dawson City, the capital, had only 819 inhabitants.

For almost 40 years after the end of the gold rush, the Yukon Territory was largely forgotten by the rest of the world, except for occasional hunters, outdoorspeople, and wilderness lovers. Then, during World War II (1939–45), faced with the threat of a Japanese invasion from the west, the U.S. government received permission from the Canadian government to build a road through Canadian territory that would connect Alaska with the lower 48 American states. In 8 months during 1942–43, more than 11,000 American soldiers and 16,000 Canadian and American civilian workers built a road across 1,445 miles (2,325 kilometers) of virgin Canadian wilderness. Now called the Alaska Highway, this all-weather road runs for 615 miles (990 kilometers) across the southwest corner of the Yukon, from Teslin on the British Columbia border through Whitehorse to Beaver Creek on the Alaska border.

Another military project that brought thousands of temporary residents to the Yukon was the Canol (Canadian Oil) Pipeline. Built during World War II, the Canol Pipeline snaked for about 620 miles (1,000 kilometers) across the Mackenzie Mountains from the oil fields of Norman Wells in the Northwest Territories to Whitehorse. The pipeline cost $134 million but operated for just one year; it shut down when the war ended in 1945.

The highway and pipeline projects brought a surge of new life to the Yukon. The territory had 9,000 residents in 1951—an increase of 100 percent since 1931. In 1953, the capital was moved from Dawson City to Whitehorse, which had a larger population and was situated on the new highway.

During the second half of the 20th century, new opportunities for employment in mining, government services, and tourism have allowed the territory's population to increase, although growth has been slow and erratic. With the help of grants and subsidies from the federal government, the Yukon managed to hold its own during the economic downturns of the 1980s.

The Northwest Territories and the Yukon Territory have a different relationship with the federal government than the Canadian provinces have. The territories have less freedom than the provinces to govern themselves; in the territories, the federal

The Alaska Highway under construction in 1942. One of the most massive road-building efforts in modern history drove the highway through 1,445 miles (2,325 kilometers) of Canadian wilderness to connect Alaska with the lower United States.

Even in the remote north, pollution and trash disposal are growing problems. Most northerners, however, want to preserve the region's beauty. Here, Whitehorse citizens clean up an old dump.

government exercises much more control over land use, natural resources, taxation, and Native affairs.

Since the 1960s, the people of the Yukon have been working toward gaining provincial status for their territory. If the Yukon became a province, its people would have more direct control over planning, resource exploitation, and other aspects of development; they would also receive a greater share of the profits from such development. Although the Yukon Territory depends on money provided by the federal government, it has gradually assumed greater responsibility for such local matters as community health, education, and resource management. In recent years the federal government has steadily allowed the territory to become more autonomous, although it has not yet granted provincial status.

The formal head of government in the Yukon Territory is a commissioner who is appointed by the federal government, but the commissioner's role is largely ceremonial; real executive power in the Yukon lies with an elected official called the government leader. The government leader is a member of the territory's 16-member elected legislative assembly and the head of the majority political party. Tony Penikett of the New Democratic party became the Yukon's government leader in 1985.

Despite steady population growth and improvement in government services since mid-century, the Yukon still faces significant challenges. One important issue that must be resolved is Native land claims. As elsewhere in Canada and the United States, Native groups in the Yukon are claiming that their homelands were taken from them without permission or fair compensation. Unlike other parts of the Americas in which Europeans ousted the Native population over a period of decades or centuries, the Yukon saw relatively little encroachment by Europeans until the end of the 19th century. No land treaty was ever offered to or signed by the Natives of the Yukon, but the Klondike gold rush of 1897–1904 and the Alaska Highway project of the 1940s brought thousands of Europeans into the territory. The towns and roads they built, and the laws they enacted, introduced swift changes into the Native way of life.

Today the Native people are attempting to reclaim their land and receive some compensation for their losses. In 1988, Penikett's government and 13 Native communities reached an agreement under which the Natives will receive $232 million and ownership of 16,600 square miles (43,000 square kilometers) of land. The details of the agreement were still being negotiated in the early 1990s.

Perhaps the biggest challenge facing the Yukon is economic development. Offshore oil production in the Beaufort Sea has been investigated as a possible source of income, but studies must first determine the potential profits from oil development as well as the potential damage to the environment. In the meantime, the territorial and federal governments must decide how the income from oil leases would be divided and used.

The Economy

The history of economic development in the Yukon is a story about transportation. Before the arrival of Europeans, people traveled by canoe on the rivers and on foot or by dogsled across the countryside—these modes of travel suited the hunting-and-gathering economy of the Native peoples. In the eyes of the Europeans who gradually spread across North America, however, the Yukon was sparsely populated and underdeveloped, doomed to isolation by its rugged terrain and remoteness from major population centers.

Modern transportation came to the Yukon with the gold rush. First, steamboats were brought north, disassembled, carried overland, reassembled, and launched on the territory's lakes and rivers. Then a railway was laid from Skagway to Whitehorse to save prospectors from having to make the perilous journey by foot over the Chilkoot Pass. The White Pass and Yukon Railway was the most steeply pitched railway in Canada when it was built. Constructing the 108-mile (175-kilometer) railway was a feat of engineering that required extensive blasting, tunneling, and bridging and a work force of more than 35,000 people.

Tourism is expected to be a major factor in the Yukon's economic future. People from elsewhere in Canada, as well as from the United States and other countries, visit the Yukon in search of wilderness experiences such as horse packing in the Firth River area (opposite) and fishing in isolated lakeside camps (above). Many parts of the territory cannot be reached by road, so bush pilots and their small planes are an important part of the transportation network.

Placer mining near Dawson City. Gold is still mined in the Yukon; much of it comes from small family-operated mines.

It has always been difficult to drive railways and roads through the Yukon, even with the advances of technology. The Alaska Highway project taught the United States and Canada a great deal about road building in the far north, and after it was completed the Canadian government launched several other ambitious highway projects in the Yukon. The Klondike Highway was begun in the 1950s. It connects Whitehorse and Dawson City; a link from Whitehorse to Skagway was completed in the 1980s. Haines Highway, completed in 1978, follows the same route as the White Pass and Yukon Railway and established the Yukon's first road access to the Pacific Ocean. The Dempster Highway to the northern coast was completed in 1979. It runs northeast from Dawson City through the Ogilvie and Richardson mountains to the coastal city of Inuvik in the Mackenzie River delta of the Northwest Territories. The Yukon now has 2,784 miles (4,480 kilometers) of highways.

New airports as well as roads were constructed in the southern Yukon during World War II. The largest, the Whitehorse airport, now provides daily scheduled and charter flights to Alaska, southern Canada, and the United States. Most communities have small airports or airstrips that are used by the bush pilots who carry passengers and freight in their small planes. The northernmost airstrip in the territory is located in Old Crow, on the banks of the Porcupine River.

Access to the Yukon has increased greatly since the late 19th century, but the territory remains somewhat isolated, both physically and economically, from the rest of Canada. The natural resources it offers—minerals, forestry products, furs, and fish—can also be found in more populated and accessible parts of the country, and operations such as mines and sawmills are often less profitable in the Yukon than elsewhere. Recent efforts to expand the resource-based economy have met with mixed success, although resource-based industries remain vital to the territory's economic survival. In recent years, many Yukoners have taken jobs in the territorial and federal governments or in service industries such as tourism, transportation, or communication. There is also a small manufacturing sector, based in the capital city of Whitehorse, that produces goods such as furniture, soft drinks, optical products, chemicals, jewelry, and outdoor gear, including wooden canoes, dogsleds, and snowshoes.

Mining

The mainstay of the economy since the gold rush, mining continues to be the most productive economic activity in the Yukon Territory. Unfortunately, the mining industry is a volatile one: The value of Yukon mineral production often varies greatly from year to year because the price for metal ores in the world marketplace fluctuates. In 1985, when metal prices were low, many Yukon mines were closed. The territory's total mineral production was valued at only about $60 million. In 1986, metal prices rose and mines reopened, driving the year's mineral production up to about $180 million. But in 1989 silver prices fell, and the United Keno Hills silver mine in Elsa, one of the Yukon's largest mining operations, was shut down, putting 170 miners out of work.

Zinc and lead have replaced gold as the most important minerals mined in the Yukon today, accounting for 45 percent and 20 percent of mining income, respectively. Silver, tungsten, and coal are also mined. But gold continues to be mined in the Yukon, and in large quantities: A century after the gold rush, the Yukon gold industry had its most profitable year ever in 1987. Gold mining accounts for approximately 22 percent of the Yukon's total mining production. About 200 placer gold mines employ a total of about 600 people each summer. These small operations, often family owned, use dredges and other equipment to recover loose gold from streambeds. The Ketza gold mine near the town of Ross River is a hard-rock mine, in which gold ore is recovered from excavated rock.

Tourism

Tourism is one of the fastest-growing sectors of the Yukon's economy, second only to mining in the amount of revenue it earns each year. It is the third largest employer, after mining and government services. In 1988, nearly 200,000 visitors spent an estimated $37 million in the territory.

Tourism got its start in the Yukon as a side effect of the gold rush, which drew the world's attention to the Yukon, as did the works of poets, novelists, and journalists who wrote about this northland. Adventure-minded travelers began to make their way into the remote region to hunt big game or visit Dawson City and other famous Klondike landmarks. Since the construction of the Yukon highways, tourism has increased dramatically, and scores of tourism-related businesses have sprung up: outfitters who organize and lead trips for hunting, fishing, river rafting and canoeing, bird-watching, or camping; hotels and wilderness lodges; and stores that sell camping supplies and Native handicrafts. Among the principal tourist attractions in the Yukon are its two large national parks, Kluane National Park in the St.

Elias Mountains and Northern Yukon National Park in the northwestern corner of the territory. The Klondike region also attracts visitors; the turn-of-the-century flavor of the gold rush still lingers in Dawson City, where many of the original buildings have been preserved. Abandoned mines, rusting dredges, ghost towns, and other relics of the past are scattered across the Klondike.

Hunting, Trapping, and Fishing

Hunting and fishing were the economic activities of the Yukon's first inhabitants. The Natives took up trapping when the fur trade reached the area in the 19th century. These activities are still very much a part of life in the Yukon. Most people—except some of those in the larger communities—hunt moose and other game for food. Trapping and fur trading provide employment for about 800 registered trappers, who harvest approximately $1 million worth of lynx, marten, beaver, muskrat, wolverine, and fox furs each year. A decline in the international fur trade since the late 1980s suggests that the fur industry in the Yukon will probably decline as well over the coming years.

A Native woman assembles padded jackets. Some Natives and Native-owned companies produce clothing and craft objects for sale to tourists and for export.

There are two types of fishing in the Yukon—sport and commercial. The sport-fishing industry earns the territory about $4 million each year from tourists who come from all over the world to catch grayling, salmon, lake trout, and northern pike. Commercial fishing in 20 lakes produces salmon, whitefish, and lake trout for local consumption or for export. The leading exporter is the Han Fisheries plant in Dawson City, operated by the Native Han people. It cans salmon and salmon caviar (eggs) for sale to Europe and Japan.

Traditional fishing methods are still maintained by many Native communities, where fish are harvested with gill nets and either dried or smoked for long-term storage. In addition, some ice fishing takes place in the winter.

Agriculture and Forestry

With little fertile soil and an extremely short growing season, the Yukon has never had a significant agricultural output. Only during the gold rush, when the need for food was overwhelming, did Yukoners try farming on a large scale. At that time, the Stewart River valley, a silver-mining region in western Canada, was used to grow crops and raise livestock to feed the mining population.

Today the Yukon has 20 agricultural businesses, 75 full-time farmers, and 25 or 30 part-time farmers. Most produce is imported, although large and delicious vegetables can be grown in greenhouses during the summer. Agricultural land is generally used to grow food for the territory's horses, dairy cattle, poultry, and sheep. The territorial government is encouraging Yukoners to become more self-sufficient through increased farming and gardening.

Forestry, like farming, is limited by the Yukon's climate. More than half of the territory is covered with boreal forest, but trees grow slowly because of the cold temperatures and the dark winters; forests do not have the dense lushness of woodlands farther south. Only 15 percent of the Yukon's forest is commercially productive, with trees that reach heights of 33 feet

Sport fishing—by both visitors and Yukoners—makes a significant contribution to the local economy.

(10 meters) or more in 100 years. The difficulty of transporting lumber and wood products to distant markets has also limited the forestry industry in the Yukon. The territory's timber operations, which are concentrated around Watson Lake, Whitehorse, and Dawson City, mainly serve local needs.

In 1987, the federal and territorial governments and private developers invested large sums to reopen a sawmill located near Watson Lake. The sawmill had declared bankruptcy and closed its doors in 1986, putting about 100 people out of work. It was reopened in 1988, but the operation lost more than $6.2 million in 1989 and was forced to close once again.

For the people of the Yukon, that sawmill has become a symbol of the ongoing economic problems that plague this isolated region with difficult terrain and a harsh climate. It suggests that large-scale economic development simply may not work in the Yukon and that perhaps the territory's capacity to sustain a population is limited. Some Yukoners and other Canadians are debating whether the Yukon can ever become economically self-sufficient, particularly if its population increases.

The People

Fewer than 30,000 people call the Yukon Territory home. They refer to the rest of the world as "the outside" and pride themselves on their individuality and hardy pioneer spirit. Yet although they live far from the major cities of Canada and the United States, the Yukoners are connected to the outside by means of satellite dishes and cable television. Radios are universal, and videocassette recorders are increasingly common. Three newspapers are published in the Yukon Territory, including a daily and a weekly in Whitehorse. Three radio stations and a TV station are based in Whitehorse as well.

People from all over the world have settled in the Yukon, but most Yukoners have come from other parts of Canada. The population includes about 5,000 Native Americans. Although there are six federal reserves—lands specifically set aside for the Native population—in the Yukon, most of the Natives live side by side with the white population. Members of the different Native groups are generally found in parts of the territory that correspond to their traditional homelands—Tlingit in the south,

Opposite: Dog sledding was once the only way to travel across deep snow. Although snowmobiles are now common in the Yukon, many people still use dogsleds for transportation and recreation. *Above:* The MacBride Museum in Whitehorse contains exhibits on the Yukon's wildlife, Native peoples, gold rush history, and mining industry.

A Native artisan displays a traditional bear mask. The Yukon's 5,000 or so Natives are striving to keep their cultures alive, to regain tribal lands, and to play a greater role in government.

around Teslin, for example, and Gwich'in in the north. Under the 1988 agreement with the territorial and federal governments, the Native peoples will not only receive title to land but will also help shape the Yukon's policies regarding land use, fish and wildlife management, and wilderness and heritage preservation.

Education and the Arts

Approximately 4,800 school-age children live in the Yukon Territory. They are educated in about 25 public schools maintained by the territorial government. Seven of these schools are high schools, located in Carmacks, Dawson City, Haines Junction, Mayo, Teslin, Watson Lake, and Whitehorse. Students from the more outlying regions who attend these schools often board with local families while school is in session.

Yukon College is the only school of higher education in the territory. Its main campus is in Whitehorse; 13 community campuses are located throughout the Yukon. It offers vocational and professional programs relating to the local economy. Students who want to go to college outside the Yukon may receive financial aid from the federal or territorial government.

Much of the Yukon's art and culture is focused on the territory's past. Six museums celebrate Yukon history; three of them are located in Whitehorse. The MacBride Museum was established in 1951 to provide an in-depth look at the Yukon's heritage through exhibits about prehistoric mammals, Native cultures, early exploration, the fur trade, the gold rush, and the Alaska Highway. The capital city also has the Yukon Transportation Museum and the Old Log Church Museum, a log church built by Anglican missionaries in the 19th century.

The George Johnston Museum in Teslin commemorates the Tlingit trapper and trader who gained international renown for his photographs of the people and events of the Yukon from the 1920s to the 1940s.

The Yukon boasts its share of well-known writers. Robert Service, a poet who wrote during the Klondike gold rush, has been called the Bard of the Yukon. In 1894, at age 20, he emigrated from England to Canada and went to work for a Canadian bank, which stationed him in Whitehorse and Dawson City. He had a front-row seat for the drama of the gold rush— one of his most popular poems, "The Shooting of Dan McGrew," is about a shoot-out in a Whitehorse saloon. Published in a volume called *The Spell of the Yukon*, the poem evokes the excitement of the Klondike. Service died in France in 1958. His cabin in Dawson City has been preserved, as has the cabin of Jack London, an American writer who lived in the Klondike during the gold rush; he wrote *The Call of the Wild* and other stirring tales of the far north.

Pierre Berton, one of Canada's best-known writers and historians, grew up in the Yukon Territory. Born in Whitehorse on July 12, 1920, Berton worked as a journalist in Vancouver before moving east to Toronto. Since then, Berton has divided his time between working in television journalism and writing books about Canadian history. His first book, *Klondike*, was about the

Carcross, a small town near Whitehorse, was once a stop on the gold rush route. Today it has fewer than 400 inhabitants, most of them Tlingit.

gold rush that made his home territory famous. Berton has received 3 Governor General's Awards and 11 honorary degrees and is a Companion of the Order of Canada.

Theater in the Yukon also draws upon the past. Actors and actresses perform nightly every summer in the Frantic Follies Vaudeville Revue in Whitehorse. With skits, songs, and high-kicking cancan dances, they bring the golden age of the Klondike to life. Similar shows are staged in Dawson City. During the winter, Guild Hall in Whitehorse presents plays and musical events, including the Frostbite Folk Festival, which features folk singers and musicians from many countries.

In recent years, efforts have been made to protect and cultivate the ancient and contemporary culture of the Yukon's Native population. Schools and government programs foster the preservation and use of Native arts, languages, and traditions. Native fine arts—particularly sculpture—have long been admired. Figures of animals, people, and spirits carved in bone and horn occupy an important niche in Native life and culture; today Native artists also sell their work to collectors from around the world.

Native Yukoners are also known for their fine leatherwork, embroidery, and beadwork. Handmade moccasins, mukluks (boots), mittens, and parkas, made from skins and embroidered with traditional designs, are functional as well as beautiful creations.

Recreation

The call of the wild is heard clearly in the Yukon, one of the last true wilderness regions of North America. Kluane National Park offers hikers 155 miles (250 kilometers) of magnificent mountain-and-lake terrain. Another hiking adventure is the gold rush trail, including the Chilkoot Pass; hundreds of people climb it each summer. Campers who visit the Northern Yukon National Park, 590 miles (944 kilometers) north of Whitehorse on the Beaufort Sea coast, may witness the massive migration of the Porcupine Plateau caribou herd. Canoeing, rafting, hunting, and wildlife-

Kluane Lake, at the edge of Kluane National Park

watching all draw residents and tourists into the vast open expanses of the Yukon.

The far north has two seasonal sporting events, each of which is held every two years: the Arctic Winter Games and the Northern Games (held in the summer). Both events attract competitors from the Yukon, the Northwest Territories, Alaska, and Greenland. The games include badminton, hockey, indoor soccer, cross-country skiing, curling, and figure skating. Traditional Native sports, which emphasize stamina and strength, are also featured at the games. These sports include the high kick, in which athletes leap as high into the air as they can, archery, tug-of-war, and wrestling.

The Communities

Only six communities in the Yukon have more than 500 inhabitants. The one large city is Whitehorse, the capital of the Yukon Territory since 1953, located about 65 miles (105 kilometers) north of the British Columbia border on the Yukon River. It is Canada's westernmost capital city and has 20,706 residents—more than two-thirds of the Yukon's population.

Nestled in a valley and protected by a circle of mountains, Whitehorse has both a beautiful cityscape and a relatively moderate climate. Its summers are particularly warm, with nearly 20 hours of sunlight every day.

Like the rest of the Yukon, Whitehorse has experienced alternating periods of boom and bust, growth and decline. During the Klondike gold rush, Whitehorse was a temporary stopping point where prospectors rested after the rigors of Miles Canyon and the Whitehorse Rapids. When the White Pass and Yukon Railway was completed in 1900, Whitehorse began to become the hub of the territory. At the junction of the river and the railroad, Whitehorse was the region's service, transportation, and employment center.

Opposite: Whitehorse, the territorial capital, is home to more than two-thirds of all Yukoners.
Above: Once the capital of the Yukon, Dawson City is today a living museum that preserves the flavor of the early-20th-century Klondike gold rush.

More than three decades of decline followed the gold rush. In 1941, the population of Whitehorse stood at just 750. But this remote, forgotten town benefited from the World War II construction projects. About 30,000 American and Canadian men and women arrived to work on the Alaska Highway and the Canol Pipeline. When the war was over and the Alaska Highway was opened to civilian traffic, Whitehorse became the headquarters of the highway system in the Canadian northwest. Because of its increased accessibility and population, Whitehorse was named capital of the territory in 1953, replacing the economically depressed and underpopulated Dawson City. Whitehorse is now the regional headquarters of the Royal Canadian Mounted Police, the successors of the NWMP, and of many federal government departments.

The past is very much a part of the present in Whitehorse, as it is throughout the Yukon. Three museums celebrate territorial history, and a trio of old paddle wheelers that once carried gold-hungry prospectors are moored in the Yukon River.

North of Whitehorse is Dawson City, which was the center of activity during the Klondike gold rush. During its heyday, Dawson City had a population of 40,000 and was called the Paris of the North. It was the capital of the Yukon to 1953.

Dawson's fortunes fell when the gold rush was over, and unlike Whitehorse, the city has never fully recovered. It remained dependent on gold mining through the mid-20th century. Since 1966, however, when the Yukon Consolidated Gold Corporation shut down its last operation in the Klondike Valley, tourism has been Dawson's primary industry. Since 1960, when Parks Canada, a federal organization, rebuilt a number of historical buildings, the city has become almost a living museum of gold rush days. The Palace Grand Theatre, built by a gold rush entrepreneur named "Arizona Charlie" Meadows, is fully restored and active. Each summer it presents the Gaslight Follies, a reenactment of life in a gold rush saloon. The Dawson City Museum, in a stately old territorial administration building, houses extensive exhibits depicting the history of the Klondike area. Dawson City's population is 1,791.

Dawson City, set among tree-clad hills and encircled by the Klondike River

Located on the Alaska Highway near the British Columbia border, the town of Watson Lake has 1,744 residents. Because it is the first town that a driver on the highway encounters in the Yukon, it is called the Gateway to the North. Named for fur trader Frank Watson, who set up a post there during the 1890s, Watson Lake is now a major transportation hub, linking roads from British Columbia with both the interior of the Yukon and the Northwest Territories.

Watson Lake's best-known feature is its signpost forest. Begun in 1942 by homesick Alaska Highway workers who posted signs pointing to their hometowns, the signpost forest grows every year, thanks to the many visitors who bring their own hometown signs to plant; it now has about 10,000 signs.

East of Dawson City are the mining towns of Mayo, Elsa, and Keno. Built on the fortunes of silver and gold, these towns have experienced the ups and downs of the mining industry. Mayo can trace its origins to 1902, when gold was discovered along the Stewart River. After the gold rush, silver deposits were found at nearby Keno Hill, and when Keno Hill Ltd., a subsidiary of the Yukon Gold Company, began mining in 1920, Mayo became a major transportation center for ore that was shipped on the Stewart River. When a road was built to connect the region to the Klondike Highway, Mayo lost its importance as the riverboat transportation hub. The nearby town of Elsa has similar roots: Silver was found there in 1924, and within five years, miners had established the village of Elsa. When mineral prices fell and mining operations closed, these mining towns lost people and businesses.

Keno was the hub of the region during the mining heyday but is almost a ghost town today: It consists of a few log structures and a small hotel. But at an elevation of 6,200 feet (1,898 meters), Keno is situated in one of the most scenic settings in the central Yukon, with a commanding view of the river and the surrounding communities.

Other Yukon communities include Faro, a mining town northeast of Whitehorse; Haines Junction, west of Whitehorse on the Alaska Highway, the entry point for Kluane National Park;

Teslin, a Tlingit community south of Whitehorse, noted for fine sport fishing; Carmacks, on the highway between Whitehorse and Dawson City and named for the man who started the gold rush; and Old Crow, the only community in the Yukon that is north of the Arctic Circle. Located on one of North America's oldest sites of human settlement, Old Crow is a Gwich'in community of about 265 people.

The boutiques and streetlamps of downtown Whitehorse offer a break from the seemingly endless vistas of earth, trees, and sky that make up the Yukon.

Things to Do and See

• **Alaska Highway Interpretive Centre,** Watson Lake: A museum devoted to the Alaska Highway. Photo murals depict the story of this World War II construction project, and the military nature of the project is highlighted by an army pyramid tent and a road construction model.

• **Watson Lake Signposts,** Watson Lake: In 1942, Carl K. Lindley of Danville, Illinois, a homesick U.S. Army soldier who was working on the construction of the Alaska Highway, put up a road sign showing the mileage and direction to his hometown. In the years that followed, hundreds of other people added their own contributions. In 1990, there were more than 10,000 signs in Watson Lake's Signpost Forest.

• **George Johnston Museum,** Teslin: A museum that celebrates the cultural heritage of the Teslin Tlingit. George Johnston was a Tlingit photographer dedicated to recording his people's culture. A selection of his early work is displayed, as are artifacts from pioneer days and the Tlingit culture.

Opposite: The Arctic Circle is crossed by travelers on the Dempster Highway, the only road into the northern Yukon. *Above:* A cyclist braves the steep gradients of the Top of the World Highway, which runs west from Dawson City into Alaska.

The Kluane Museum of Natural History in Burwash Landing features wildlife displays and Native handicrafts.

- **Kluane Park Headquarters,** Haines Junction: Located just off the Alaska Highway, this small museum offers an award-winning video describing Kluane National Park, Canada's largest mountain park and a United Nations World Heritage Site.

- **Frontierland Theme Park,** Carcross: A theme park located beside the Museum of Yukon Natural History. Gold panning is one of the attractions.

- **Museum of Yukon Natural History,** Carcross: Specimens of Yukon wildlife mounted in dioramas that portray the variety of natural habitats in the territory.

- **Duncan Creek Golddusters,** Mayo: A guided tour of a family mining and panning operation shows how new technology has changed mining operations since the gold rush days.

- **Keno Mining Museum,** Keno City: This museum was established by a small group of dedicated volunteers intent on preserving the history of one of Canada's most important silver-mining areas. A large gallery displays blacksmithing tools, mining implements, old photographs, archives, and other memorabilia.

- **Palace Grand Theatre,** Dawson City: Originally built by a well-known entrepreneur named "Arizona Charlie" Meadows in 1899, this reconstructed turn-of-the-century theater showcases the Gaslight Follies, a variety show presented in turn-of-the-century style, with music, songs, dances, and colorful costumes.

• **Robert Service Cabin,** Dawson City: The cabin where poet Robert Service, the Bard of the Yukon, lived during the early 20th century. Service penned the Canadian classics "The Cremation of Sam McGee" and "The Shooting of Dan McGrew" while living there.

• **Jack London's Cabin and Interpretation Centre,** Dawson City: Jack London, an American novelist and the author of *White Fang* and *The Call of the Wild,* once lived here. Readings from his works are presented daily, and his experiences in the Klondike are depicted in an extensive photo exhibit.

• **Dawson City Museum,** Dawson City: A renovated turn-of-the-century building with two galleries and a number of smaller displays. Exhibits depict Klondike history and Native culture. A reference center assists historical researchers interested in the territory's past.

• **MacBride Museum,** Whitehorse: Archaeological, cultural, historical, transportation, and mining exhibits are located in the W. D. MacBride Centennial Museum, the Yukon's only museum open all year.

• **Yukon Transportation Museum,** Whitehorse: Located on the Alaska Highway, this museum displays the types of transportation used in the Yukon's rugged terrain, including Native boats and snowshoes, dogsleds, and a full-size replica of the first commercial aircraft in the Yukon.

• **Yukon Gardens,** Whitehorse: Large displays of wild plants, hardy vegetables, fruit trees, and commercial flowers. Added attractions are an international bird collection and a garden shopping center where plants are for sale.

• **Yukon Wildlife Preserve,** Whitehorse: Animals roam freely in this preserve, which covers hundreds of acres of forests, meadows, and marshlands. Inhabitants include elk, caribou, bison, moose, mountain goats, snowy owls, and rare peregrine falcons.

Festivals

Southern Lakes Classic Dogsled Race, Carcross, beginning of February: A two-day round-trip dogsled race between the tiny towns of Carcross and Tagish.

Frostbite Music Festival, Whitehorse, mid-February: Two days of music workshops, concerts, and evening dances. Musicians and entertainers come from all over Canada and the United States to perform.

Annual Yukon Quest, end of February: Top dogsled mushers from across North America compete for a $50,000 purse in this 1,000-mile (1,600-kilometer) dogsled race from Whitehorse to Fairbanks, Alaska. Spectators flock to Whitehorse, Carmacks, and Dawson City to watch the race.

International Curling Bonspiel, Whitehorse, end of March: One hundred teams compete for $10,000 in cash and prizes in a 4-day bonspiel, or curling tournament, hosted by the Whitehorse Curling Club.

International Gold Show, Dawson City, end of May: An annual trade show and seminar on placer mining for gold.

Opposite: Dancers at Diamond Tooth Gertie's Gambling Hall in Dawson City reenact the high-kicking days of the Klondike gold rush.
Above: A contestant tries her skill at log sawing during the Discovery Day festival in Dawson City.

Sourdough Stompers Square and Round Dance Jamboree,
Whitehorse, beginning of May: Square dancers from the Yukon,
Alaska, and western Canada kick up their heels at this annual
event in the territorial capital.

Northern Storytelling Festival, Whitehorse, beginning of June:
Native and traditional stories from the Arctic and the Canadian
north are told by expert raconteurs.

Yukon Gold Panning Championships, Dawson City, July 1:
Yukon residents compete to see who can retrieve the most gold
by panning, or sifting water-borne sediment to reveal nuggets and
dust. Visitors compete for a separate prize.

Annual Dawson City Music Festival, Dawson City, mid-July:
Entertainers and artists from Canada and the United States hold
music workshops, concerts, and dances.

The Signpost Forest at Watson Lake contains 10,000 signs that have been brought from all over the world during the latter half of the 20th century.

Camping on the tundra

Canada Day Celebrations, throughout the territory, July 1: Outdoor concerts, softball tournaments, a fishing derby, and many other events and traditional games are held to honor the day Canada became a nation.

Yukon Indian Days, Teslin Lake, end of July: All groups of Yukon Natives join together every summer to celebrate their cultures and traditions through music, art, and dance.

Discovery Day, Dawson City, mid-August: The day gold was discovered in the Klondike (August 17, 1896) is commemorated every year with a festival that includes parades, raft and canoe races, ball games, dances, and many other events.

The Great Klondike Outhouse Race, Dawson City, beginning of September: Outhouses on wheels race more than 1.5 miles (2.4 kilometers) through the streets of Dawson City.

Chronology

by A.D. 800	The Native American Athapaskan culture is well established in the Yukon.
1840s	John Bell and Robert Campbell of the Hudson's Bay Company explore the interior and establish trading posts.
1867	The United States buys Alaska from Russia. The Dominion of Canada gains independence from Britain.
1869	Canada acquires the territory that includes the Yukon.
1895	The Canadian government establishes the Yukon administrative district.
1896	Gold is discovered in Bonanza Creek near the Klondike River.
1897	The Klondike gold rush begins.
1898	The Yukon is given territorial status.
1900	The White Pass and Yukon Railway from Skagway, Alaska, to Whitehorse, Yukon, is completed.
by 1904	The gold rush has ended. The Yukon's fortunes and population begin to decline.
1942–43	The Alaska Highway is built through the southwestern Yukon.
1953	Whitehorse is made the territorial capital.
1988	The Native peoples and the federal and territorial governments reach an agreement on land claims and administrative participation.
1992	The Yukon celebrates the 50th anniversary of the construction of the Alaska Highway.

Further Reading

Berton, Pierre. *Drifting Home.* New York: Knopf, 1974.

Cantin, Eugene. *Yukon Summer.* San Francisco: Chronicle Books, 1973.

Hildebrand, John. *Reading the River: A Voyage Down the Yukon.* New York: Houghton Mifflin, 1988.

Hocking, Anthony. *The Yukon and the Northwest Territories.* New York: McGraw-Hill Ryerson, 1979.

Holbrook, Sara. *Canada's Kids.* New York: Atheneum, 1983.

Hope, Jack. *Yukon.* Englewood Cliffs, NJ: Prentice-Hall, 1976.

Law, Kevin. *Canada.* New York: Chelsea House, 1990.

McNaught, Kenneth. *The Penguin History of Canada.* New York: Penguin Books, 1988.

Malcolm, Andrew. *The Canadians.* New York: Random House, 1985.

Mathews, Richard K. *The Yukon.* New York: Holt, Rinehart & Winston, 1968.

Satterfield, Archie. *After the Gold Rush.* Philadelphia: Lippincott, 1976.

Webb, Melody. *The Last Frontier.* Albuquerque: University of New Mexico Press, 1985.

Woodcock, George. *The Canadians.* Cambridge: Harvard University Press, 1979.

Index

ACKNOWLEDGMENTS

Diana Blume: p. 6; Phil A. Dotson/Photo Researchers: p. 9; R. Hartmier: cover; Industry, Science and Technology, Canada: pp. 8, 14, 32, 34, 37, 42, 46, 49, 51, 57, 59; Steve Kraseman/Photo Researchers: p. 58; National Archives of Canada: pp. 16 (neg. # C14474), 17 (neg. # C22074), 21 (neg. # C1352), 23 (neg. # PA45109), 26 (neg. # PA44683), 29 (neg. # C7489); National Museums of Canada: pp. 18 (neg. # 51657), 20 (neg. # J-806), 25 (neg. # J-6078), 27 (neg. # J-6271); Debora Smith: p. 7; Mike Thomas/ *Whitehorse Star:* p. 30; Yukon government photo: pp. 3, 5, 11, 12, 33, 39, 40, 41, 43, 45, 47, 52, 53, 54, 56

Suzanne LeVert has contributed several volumes to Chelsea House's LET'S DISCOVER CANADA series. She is the author of four previous books for young readers. One of these, *The Sakharov File*, biography of noted Russian physicist Andrei Sakharov, was selected as a Notable Book by the National Council for the Social Studies. Her other books include *AIDS: In Search of a Killer, The Doubleday Book of Famous Americans*, and *New York*. Ms. LeVert also has extensive experience as an editor, first in children's books at Simon & Schuster, then as associate editor at *Trialogue*, the magazine of the Trilateral Commission, and as senior editor at Save the Children, the international relief and development organization. She lives in Cambridge, Massachusetts.

George Sheppard, General Editor, is a lecturer on Canadian and American history at McMaster University in Hamilton, Ontario. Dr. Sheppard holds an honors B.A. and an M.A. in history from Laurentian University and earned his Ph.D. in Canadian history at McMaster. He has taught Canadian history at Nipissing University in North Bay. His research specialty is the War of 1812, and he has published articles in *Histoire sociale/Social History, Papers of the Bibliographical Society of Canada*, and *Ontario History*. Dr. Sheppard is a native of Timmins, Ontario.

Pierre Berton, Senior Consulting Editor, is the author of 34 books, including *The Mysterious North, Klondike, Great Canadians, The Last Spike, The Great Railway Illustrated, Hollywood's Canada, My Country: The Remarkable Past, The Wild Frontier, The Invasion of Canada, Why We Act Like Canadians, The Klondike Quest*, and *The Arctic Grail*. He has won three Governor General's Awards for creative nonfiction, two National Newspaper Awards, and two ACTRA "Nellies" for broadcasting. He is a Companion of the Order of Canada, a member of the Canadian News Hall of Fame, and holds 12 honorary degrees. Raised in the Yukon, Mr. Berton began his newspaper career in Vancouver. He then became managing editor of *McLean's*, Canada's largest magazine, and subsequently worked for the Canadian Broadcasting Network and the *Toronto Star*. He lives in Kleinburg, Ontario.